SYMBOLS OF AMERICAN FREEDOM

The Bald Eagle

by Mari Schuh

BLASTOFF! READERS

BELLWETHER MEDIA • MINNEAPOLIS, MN

Note to Librarians, Teachers, and Parents:

Blastoff! Readers are carefully developed by literacy experts and combine standards-based content with developmentally appropriate text.

Level 1 provides the most support through repetition of high-frequency words, light text, predictable sentence patterns, and strong visual support.

Level 2 offers early readers a bit more challenge through varied simple sentences, increased text load, and less repetition of high-frequency words.

Level 3 advances early-fluent readers toward fluency through increased text and concept load, less reliance on visuals, longer sentences, and more literary language.

Level 4 builds reading stamina by providing more text per page, increased use of punctuation, greater variation in sentence patterns, and increasingly challenging vocabulary.

Level 5 encourages children to move from "learning to read" to "reading to learn" by providing even more text, varied writing styles, and less familiar topics.

Whichever book is right for your reader, Blastoff! Readers are the perfect books to build confidence and encourage a love of reading that will last a lifetime!

This edition first published in 2019 by Bellwether Media, Inc.

No part of this publication may be reproduced in whole or in part without written permission of the publisher. For information regarding permission, write to Bellwether Media, Inc., Attention: Permissions Department, 6012 Blue Circle Drive, Minnetonka, MN 55343.

Library of Congress Cataloging-in-Publication Data

LC record for The Bald Eagle available at https://lccn.loc.gov/2017061641

Editor: Rebecca Sabelko   Designer: Andrea Schneider

Printed in the United States of America, North Mankato, MN.

Table of Contents

What Is a Bald Eagle?

The bald eagle is an American **symbol** of **freedom**. It stands for strength and **courage**.

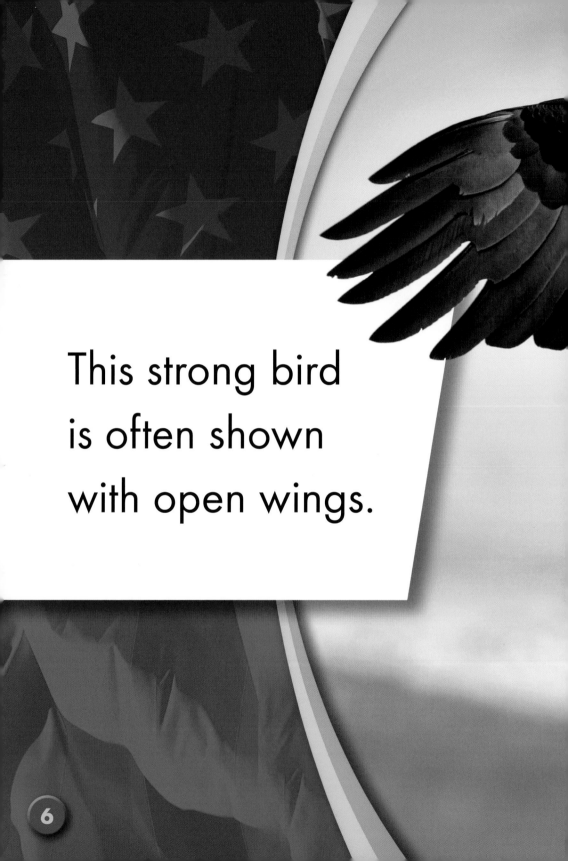

This strong bird
is often shown
with open wings.

The bald eagle is the national bird. It only lives in North America.

National Symbol

The **founders** of America wanted a **seal**.

The **Great Seal** shows the bald eagle. It was made in 1782.

Parts of the Seal

olive branch stands for peace

arrows stand for war

13 stripes on the shield stand for America's first 13 colonies

In 1787, the bald eagle became the national bird.

A Symbol of Freedom

Today, the bald eagle is on coins. It is on dollar bills, too.

quarter

Stamps and flags also show the bald eagle.

The bald eagle
is America's bird.
It flies free!

Glossary

courage

bravery

Great Seal

the mark of the United States government

founders

the men who helped the first thirteen colonies become a country

seal

a mark, stamp, or design for a person or group

freedom

the state of being free

symbol

something that stands for something else

To Learn More

AT THE LIBRARY
Ferguson, Melissa. *American Symbols: What You Need to Know*. North Mankato, Minn.: Capstone Press, 2018.

Nelson, Maria. *The Bald Eagle*. New York, N.Y.: Gareth Stevens Publishing, 2015.

Rustad, Martha E.H. *Is a Bald Eagle Really Bald?* Minneapolis, Minn.: Millbrook Press, 2015.

ON THE WEB
Learning more about the bald eagle is as easy as 1, 2, 3.

1. Go to www.factsurfer.com.

2. Enter "bald eagle" into the search box.

3. Click the "Surf" button and you will see a list of related web sites.

With factsurfer.com, finding more information is just a click away.

Index

The images in this book are reproduced through the courtesy of: Chris Hill, front cover; Serjio74, p. 3; FloridaStock, pp. 4-5, 6-7, 16-17; KenCanning, pp. 8-9; Archive Images/ Alamy, pp. 10-11; Kichigin, pp. 12-13; blurAZ, p. 13; Tamer Desouky, pp. 14-15; Fat Jackey, p. 17; Stuart Monk, pp. 18-19; cvrestan, pp. 20-21; Bumble Dee, p. 22 (top left); Monkey Business Images, p. 22 (bottom right); vkilikov, p. 22 (top right); djedzura, p. 22 (middle right); fstop123, p. 22 (bottom left); The Indian Reporter/ Wiki Commons, p. 22 (middle left).